Vertically Coastal

Vertically Coastal

POEMS BY

Jerri Chaplin

EDITED AND
INTRODUCED BY

Dan Valenti

PLANET
MEDIA
BOOKS

ÉUROPOLIS

VERTICALLY COASTAL
Poems by Jerri Chaplin, edited and introduced by Dan Valenti

Copyright © 2011 by Jerri Chaplin and Dan Valenti

Planet Media Books, founded by Dan Valenti in 2010, publishes works from new and established authors in a wide range of topics, including poetry, spirituality, art, philosophy, politics, economics, cooking, essays, nonfiction, and genre fiction. The press emphasizes creativity, fresh thought, quality writing, and ideas of important merit. Planet Media Books is an imprint of Planet Valenti (planetvalenti.com) in association with Európolis Management.

ISBN: 978-1-61468-032-1

Cover concept by Dan Valenti
Cover and book design by Melissa Mykal Batalin

Printed in the United States of America
The Troy Book Makers • Troy, New York • thetroybookmakers.com

Additional copies of this title available at planetvalenti.com, danvalenti@verizon.net, tmbbooks.com, amazon.com, your local bookstore, and Planet Media Books, c/o Európolis Management, PO Box 1268, Stockbridge, MA 01262

DEDICATION

To Peter,
*who for 26 years has selflessly put me first;
loved, cherished, and comforted me;
and has helped tremendously
in every aspect of my life.
Thank you.*

IN MEMORIAM

Ayzck Chaplinski,
deceased at age 2, Poland.
Akiba Chaplinski,
baby, deceased at sea.
Kalani Durdan,
childhood friend, gone too soon.

ACKNOWLEDGMENTS

With thanks to:

Dan Valenti — Publisher, editor, professor, author, broadcaster, journalist, reader, blogger, and critic. You applied all your talents to my work. Thank you for your belief in my poetry, your gentle constructive criticism, and your excellent communication. You said it would be fun. You were right!

Dan Leven, for teaching me to roar between dance steps.

Rebecca Stimac, Charleston, and Alayne Glass, Pittsfield, for enabling me to live vertically coastal.

My sweet sheltie, forever dog Phoenix

CONTENTS

JERRI CHAPLIN:

FROM THE ACTUAL,
NOT THE ABSTRACT

The truism happens to be true: The shorter the word count, the more difficult the writing. Most non-writers don't understand that and fewer believe. Nonetheless, those who write for a living know that lengthy word counts allow for rhetorical wiggle room when vexing ideas out of pure conceptual form and onto the crudities of "the page." In this transubstantiation, much gets lost.

The loose confines of prose can accommodate this wiggle room with relative ease, especially as word counts go up. What full-length novel does not rattle with ideas that didn't quite make it out the way the author meant to give birth? As you recede in length, though, the room for error diminishes. Short story, essay, poem: the fewer the words, the more each one must bear of the meaning. For this reason, William Carlos Williams' "Red Wheelbarrow" might arguably stand as the greatest poem of all time.

Plato, it turns out, latched onto something useful when he gave us the allegory of the cave. An actual hammer never matches the mind's ideal hammer. If we can imagine it, we can never build it the same, a dictum, incidentally, that many movie directors don't "get" who load their films with "realistic" computerized special effects. They (or their writers) can imagine anything. It doesn't mean "anything" should get filmed. Give me the special effects pre-computer any day, those of Doug Trumbull, for instance, resident of the Berkshires who gave Stanley Kubrick miracles in *2001: A Space Odyssey* all those years ago.

So little "good" poetry is being written because it's so difficult to write. T.S. Eliot famously told us "between the idea and the reality falls the shadow." The "shadow" also falls "between the motions and the act." I interpret this in connection with the writing process. Most people live incredibly rich conceptual lives, but who among us can faithfully translate the depth of thought into the shallowness of the printed page without serious loss — or even worse, try to move the mind's ideas to the non-existent physicality of electronic blips organized in the vastness and nowhere-ness of cyberspace.

Two other poets were more direct than Eliot in trying to explain the arduousness of writing good poems. W.H. Auden complained that "poetry made nothing happen." Marianne Moore wrote of poetry "I, too, dislike it." They weren't bashing their craft (the opposite, in fact). Rather, Auden and Moore were master poets addressing the problem of confronting their work on the page?

No matter how brilliantly they wrote, when compared to their conceptualizations, the work of these two great writers typically disappointed their authors. That their readers thought otherwise made no difference and provided little comfort. The "idea" and the "reality" didn't match up, and this dissonance comprises the silent pain writers must usually endure. Readers never catch on. Readers, bless them, receive the gifts of creation fully formed and have little to no notion of the conception of those gifts.

In addition to the tremendous thrill, probably every writer has some regrets when reading his or her work in published form. When reading something already published and frozen on the page, the writer will have to guard against the temptation to second guess his or her final choices, no doubt the result of many rewrites. Reading published lines can easily cause regret that he or she didn't find a more artful way to express the thought. Always, there are better words than the ones you use.

You can imagine, then, when out of the slush pile comes a poetry manuscript that exceeds expectations and springs forth to make demands on the editor's time and attention. You get where I'm going: I'm going on a journey from Charleston, S.C., to the famed

Berkshire Hills in western Massachusetts to arrive at the book you hold in your hands: *Vertically Coastal* by Jerri Chaplin.

Every accomplished book lives three lives. The first exists as the manuscript child (man-child) in the Promised Land of the author mind's. It becomes born again (and borne again) when it takes book form from the author's execution. There, whether it's physically bound or all aglow and Kindled, the book grows into maturity capable of affecting the lives of readers. That is its second life. Finally, once again it resurrects. The message of the book begins its work of changing, shaping, and influencing the reader's understanding of his or her world. That's when a book comes alive, when it completes the journey as a conceptual creation in the author's mind and ends up as a thought or idea in the reader's.

When that happens, words attain explosive power. Lenin, as most dictators do, caught on quickly. The first thing he did when taking power was to ban freedom of the press. He explained it by saying words were far more dangerous than guns and bullets. These are the kinds of words that have started wars and stopped them.

For me, *Vertically Coastal* took the opportunity of that third life to meld into mine, not to start a war but to extend a peace. If I had been a reader of this book, I would have bought it, instantly. As it turned out, I was its potential editor and publisher. I did more than pay cover price for a work of art. I decided to play venture capitalist and help bring this work of art to life, putting my money where most put their mouth. It became the third book signed and published by Planet Media Books. In short, as I spent time with Chaplin's manuscript, I came to believe in it and in her.

As I got familiar with Jerri Chaplin's voice in *Vertically Coastal*, I began to get the clear sense of her Meaning. Sorry for using a capital "M," but the question of "What's it add up to?" requires the 13th letter of the alphabet's promotion to initial Upper Case. We kick "M" upstairs to find its fullest level of competence. Call it the Danny Principle (Jerri has her own Peter principal. He's her husband!)

Meaning, via the medium, is the message. Film mogul Louis B. Mayer, ever the commercial hawk, said that if you want to send a message, go to Western Union. Mayer uttered that philistine *Bartlett's* quotation in response to critics who knocked MGM's tendency to produce celluloid cotton candy for the masses, avoiding relevance, controversy, or important issues.

A book is far different than a movie. A book must contain a message, alternately called the "theme" or "controlling idea."

So what's the message of *Vertically Coastal*? I will not say, and not for fear of having to publish a "spoiler alert." As a critic, I don't hesitate to spoil the ending if it's necessary to make my point. As editor and publisher, however, I should be the last person to address this question of "meaning." Having lived and wrestled with this manuscript for several months, yes, I do know the "message," but I won't share it outright.

Why should I take away the reader's greatest joy? Why should I pre-program the reader to find "X" in *Vertically Coastal*? Why would I solve the mystery of the book ahead of time? Doing that would make me guilty of taking the "Perry Mason" or "Columbo" approach to the pleasure and appreciation of art. Sadly, it seems that more and more people — perhaps numbed by their blur-fast technology and unwilling to think for themselves in the wash of the eternal hurry — want to wear this type of directional nose ring.

Remember those two TV shows? Those of certain generations will. Each episode involved a murder mystery, usually beginning by showing how the crime occurred and "whodunit." This timeworn narrative gimmick focuses the audience's attention not on solving the crime but on watching how the criminal gets caught. We are tricked into appreciating the genius of the heroics and the goodness of the heroes. Mason never loses a case and Lt. Columbo always nabs the bad guy or gal. We marvel as they brilliantly force a confession from the real killer.

There's no criminal activity going on in *Vertically Coastal*, of course, but to reveal here the book's controlling idea would focus too much of the reader's attention on how Jerri Chaplin "got there" as a writer. That would not be criminal but close.

Therefore, as an expert on this book, I advise that you approach these poems on your own and as you wish. I feel honor-bound not to coax readers, since reading is such a personal act, and I say it straight: I love readers. Follow your instincts and sensibilities. Relax. Embrace the messages and the mysteries. Open yourself up to the individual poems and let them "speak" to you. If you do that, you cannot miss the "message," which will be the one you are intended to receive.

Best of all, the poems will tell you something they can't say to anyone else, for as readers, you are island universes unto yourselves, a point we will revisit momentarily.

We have divided *Vertically Coastal* into two sections: one each on Charleston, S.C., and The Berkshires. A transitional poem — from which this collection takes its name — serves as the bridge that takes us from Part One to Part Three. When I was working with this manuscript, I visualized each of the two parts as structural steel beams, fastened together by a rivet that went into matching holes of two overlapping end tabs. That rivet is the title poem.

Jerri and her husband spend time alternately in Charleston and The Berkshires, from late fall to early spring "down there" and then early spring to late fall "up here." South to North, then North to South: The poet's dual residency has shaped two reciprocal experiences of locale that together form a unified whole. The title *Vertically Coastal* describes how the writer has come to experience her world as inspired by and lived in cities at these two "coastal" locations.

"Coastal," the title says.

Charleston, with its pastel spouts and smoky tides lapping the waters of the Atlantic, doesn't need the quotes. Charleston, S.C., is as coastal as the sea foam of the ocean's crashing waves. The landlocked Berkshires — roughly equidistant 125 miles north of New York City and 125 west of Boston — can be considered "coastal" in terms of Jerri and Peter's journey to and fro, when they travel along the Atlantic seaboard from one location to the other.

Chaplin's poems, though, aren't about journeys but about destinations. To paraphrase Robert Louis Stevenson, Chaplin writes about *having arrived* more than *traveling hopefully*. Her hope can be found when she "gets there." The biannual trip from Charleston, S.C., to Pittsfield, Mass., serves as the channel that transports her from one life to the other. Like a saint of old, she's known for the art of bi-location. Yes, readers, there is no end to the poet's ability.

The poems in *Vertically Coastal* address the lives she lives in each of these beautiful locations. These two lives are existential dualities that unite in her to make the person she is, was, and will be.

It's also telling that she has a tendency to live in beautiful places. Having spent much of her young life in Hawaii, she now resides a half-year each in Charleston — a sunny, Southern, sea-city that conjures images "of the times that were // And scarce have ceased to be" (Shelley, "The Triumph of Life," lines 233 and 234) — and the Berkshires, a verdant cultural Mecca of the art and artists, a land that has "long outlived both woes and wars" (line 266). Each destination becomes the locale that shapes her voice. Like intersecting circles, they overlap.

Perhaps unique among the characteristics of poetry stands the attribute of voice. Yes, every piece of writing regardless of form contains the writer's voice, but no form magnifies that quality the way poetry does. If the printed page is poetry's physical medium, voice is its rhetorical channel. Prose has vocal considerations, surely, but the matter of word length again comes into question. With fewer words, poetry must still pack the same amount of meaning or more as much longer prose works.

This raises poetry's Quotient of Meaning Per Word to an artistically daunting degree. The accomplished poet must communicate without wasting a single syllable or mark on the page. Most poetry today resembles Dr. Johnson's observation of a bear walking on its hind legs: "It is not done well, but it's remarkable that it should be done at all." Vertically Coastal not only walks well but dances. Consequently, the poet's voice has nowhere to hide. If it's not "There" and immediately apparent …

I let this sentence tail off into nowhere, having read too much lousy poetry with no voice at all except for fear, which a writer expresses through timidity and tenuousness. I can see that fear in a poem in a glance and taste it bitterly with just a thimble full.

Voice, closely related to style, comprises the writer's literary fingerprint. On the page, words look the same, excepting the unique architectural arrangements poetry allows (think, for example, of seeing e.e. cummings on the page). The words' meaning conveys the author's unique vision. Like fingerprints, no two authorial visions are alike, though at first glance all words look the same.

Jerri Chaplin's poetry tends toward the descriptive more than the evocative, that is, she invokes feelings from her arrangement of *the actual* as it unfolds in her day-to-day life. She doesn't start with the abstract but with the tangible, extracting meaning "from the earth" to end up "in the sky."

She focuses her attention on the most extraordinary topic of all: the "ordinary." Hers is the papaya and pomegranate resting together on the kitchen counter, the slow-motion deterioration of an old barn, or a baby dancing in the dizzy joy of first-infant movement. Chaplin juxtaposes these vignettes from everyday life in relation to her delicate sensibility. She takes the tangible and the abstract, rubs them together with verbal zest, and creates rhetorical fire from people we can see, objects we can hold, and places we can visit.

Physical objects, actual people and events, and existing places come first in Chaplin's poems because they come first to her attention. There's no trickery or affectation going on in these poems. She's showing you who she is and why she is that way.

Most artists *notice* the "every day." Non-artists do not. My mom and dad, both 90 years old, have stayed young by noticing significance in the mundane. They weren't "artists" in the Picasso or Hemingway sense. Dad retired as a toolmaker and mom from a factory job. They are artists nonetheless. To them, the mundane contains the miraculous. That's why she still chases him around the house in their 68th year of marriage.

Through the actual, Chaplin doesn't "tell" us who she is. She shows us. The "actual" could be the lay of a Charleston landscape or the *chiaroscuro* of a Berkshire glade. It could be the eerie shadow a tree casts during an eclipse. From the actual, Chaplin invokes the emotions, almost (not quite) avoiding the overly dense and conceptual (think, maybe, of a radical application of Eliot's *objective correlative*).

Let me paint with broad strokes here and present another analogy to help you approach Chaplin's work. All writing can be divided into two categories: prose and poetry. Poetry, more roughly, can similarly be divided into two affective sections: poets who are "redskins" (think William Blake, e.e. cummings, and Alan Ginsberg) or "palefaces" (T.S. Eliot, Ezra Pound, and Wallace Stevens).* Chaplin is more the former. She's the earth more than the sky.

Chaplin's "physicality" produces genuine emotions, defined as states of being that are not internally counterfeited. A pure emotion can never be manufactured for the purpose of self-deception; it can only be created for the exploitation of others or perhaps for their own good. One can fool others by faking a laugh as a polite response to an unfunny joke, releasing a phony cry to gain sympathy, or sharing a shard of affected compassion to give the illusion that one cares. However, one can never fool oneself. For instance, if you fake crocodile tears to get attention, the other person may not catch on but you will certainly know, and then where are you? You are inside a "cry" that may as well be the self-indictment of a mocking laugh.

---

* Strictly as an aside, I would invite anyone who wishes to raise objections to these two categories by appealing to "political correctness" to wrap their lips around the exhaust pipe of an idling bus and inhale deeply. My apologies, O, my brothers and sisters, but such are the warnings that must be issued in an age when free speech cowers from the ugly assaults of the loony Left and the rabid Right, polar opposites that shall be taxed to a vein-popping decree in the 2012 presidential elections and those of the foreseeable future.

Let's now return to the reader's place in all this. Every reader brings an exclusive, unrepeated, and unrepeatable collection of life and experience into the activity of scanning words on a page for the purpose of decoding their meaning. The reader completes the writer's artistic task, which is, essentially, to communicate. Writer and reader form a partnership as real as Laurel and Hardy, Ben and Jerry's, or Brady-to-Welker.

The writer sends. The reader receives. The first is active, and the second is passive. The reader's reception, though, constitutes one of the most unusual forms of passivity possible. Especially with poetry, to gain the full pleasure of the experience, readers must take what they receive and put it to use.

A little recognized fact of reading has to do with identity. As we have seen, when an author pens words, they reveal much of who they are. Readers, too, risk a confrontation with identity, although — compared to that of a published writer's — it's far less intense and way more private.

Has a writer deliberately written something that provokes you into anger? Has she moved you to laughter or triggered regrets over some ancient sin? Has he thrilled you with adventure? Anytime this happens, the reader reacts as a consequence of working up his or her personal psycho-emotional profile. Readers bring all of who they are and all of what they have into the activity, and that's the only way for reading to become a joy. Could that be the reason why reading seems to interest fewer people or why those who do read tend to prefer the veneer of Danielle Steele's sex-and-shopping novels to the depth of, say, anything by Octavio Paz?

A child can only learn to read with proficiency when he or she can slow down, focus, and be willing to bring everything they have into the task. In this day of the omnipresent and omnipotent smart phone and the blinding rapidity and distraction of Twitter, can we expect children to want to learn, then regularly practice, this slow, deliberate joy masquerading as a chore? Let us hope so.

In light of the intense, personal nature of reading, the question to ask in the interpretation of a text — or any work of art, for that matter — is never: "What does it mean"? The proper question is: "What does it mean *to you*"? What I find funny someone else might find a dud. What saddens me might gladden another.

Nonetheless, about the poems of *Vertically Coastal*, we can confidently generalize. You will experience them as genuine. You won't find a disingenuous molecule in Jerri Chaplin's work. It's not to say you will enjoy her work, but at minimum you will meet and greet authenticity. When that occurs in writing, voice refines itself into tone, a quality that unambiguously conveys the writer's feelings toward the topic. Is Chaplin happy, sad, wistful, appreciative, strident, laid back, angry, or gentle? That determination, my dear readers, is tone. Read the poems, and you will know.

Tone is based on diction, defined as the writer's choice of words. The English language is blessed with a richness of words, particularly verbs. One of the best things people can do is to expand their vocabulary, even if you're not a writer or speaker. Learning more words enables a person to apply a greater range of rhetorical options when trying to match thought to speaking or writing. For a writer, a large vocabulary is as necessary as a chain saw is to an arborist.

Great poetry must by definition have the greatest diction of any kind of writing. There's too much riding on each word of a poem to allow much deadwood. Does the word do its job? If so, it stays. If not, it goes. Both writer as revisionist and editor as shaper must be ruthless in this judgment.

Let me give you a great example of diction, this in Chaplin's poem "Charlie at the Carriage," where she writes of a dying horse. She describes this gentle animal in his heart-wrenching last throes. On Christmas Eve, we see Charlie "collapsing on a Charleston street."

The horse "collapses."

It doesn't fall or drop. It doesn't buckle, crumble, or slump.

It "collapses."

Why?

You might explain it away as an arbitrary choice by the author. You would be wrong. Regardless of how much time Chaplin actually spent finding this word to describe what she saw — it could have come to her in the next second or maybe a year later — she made a deliberate, strategic choice.

The word "collapsing" suggests more than any of the alternatives Charlie's uncomplaining, heroic resolution to hold on, hold-hold on, hold-hold-hold on to life, until he can no longer support his one-ton weight. Then he goes, all of a sudden, "collapsing" as a whole to the ground, like Jesus falling under the cross for the third time on the way to Golgotha.

Another example may be more familiar. In George Orwell's famous essay "Shooting an Elephant," the author describes the animal's death in a way you will never forget. For most of the essay's finale, Orwell lingers unsparingly at the elephant's suffering.

When the elephant finally begins to go down after Orwell has emptied his rifle, it "sags." It doesn't "collapse," as does Chaplin's Charlie. "Sags" suggests a much slower fall. When the elephant loses control of its bodily functions, its mouth opens to a "cavernous" size. "Cavern" suggests the enormity of the elephant. These words are perfect examples of diction.

Back to Charlie: When the horse collapses, "Its ambitious weight," Chaplin writes, "will crush its own organs — large, meaty, fragile // as red internal flowers — // in a silent, unconscious suicide, cannibalism without teeth, // dying, dumb, and unknowing."

Charlie dies a death that rends the heart. "Collapsing" — what the perfect word!

Chaplin's poetry throughout *Vertically Coastal* springs these emotions loose from the actualities of her day-to-day lives in the Charleston South and the Berkshire North. For instance, in "South Carolina Connections," she presents an image of people sitting "on someone's piazza, drinking sweet tea, sharing stories about those they love and hate, often the same person." Up North, in the Berkshires in summer, you hear musicians practicing, "Symphony players" whose notes pass through the poet's "raspberry-growing Berkshire backyard."

In the first example, who cannot feel the lazy ambiguousness of a far-too-interconnected family of gossipers? They sit on "someone's porch." The anonymity suggests the author's attitude toward the inconsequentiality of the busybodies. In the second example, who cannot feel time slow down to summer or taste the air-fresh sweetness of a ripe raspberry? Who will not respond warmly, cozily, to the delightful images of soothing music and ripe fruit?

This leads to another consideration, nearly exclusive to poetry. It matters greatly how the poet arranges her words on the page. Writers of consecutive prose do not need to bother with this headache. The "proser" starts a paragraph, completes the idea, and then hits the tab key to begin the next paragraph. Done. On the other hand, the poet must not only get the right words but also place them graphically in the right arrangement.

After examining the words, most of my work on this book consisted of checking the placement of literally e-v-e-r-y-t-h-i-n-g. I won't get into much detail here for fear of giving you more "inside baseball" than you care to know, but allow a few observations.

The free-verse poems in *Vertically Coastal* run ragged-right on the page, suggesting the ebb and flow of tidal life shared by every living creature or created thing (the ups and downs, the triumphs and failures). We could have set them flush right, but that would have produced too much odd spacing and would have had the effect of placing words in the straightjacket of aligned left and right margins.

Technically, Chaplin's poems are "irregular" in form, meaning the poet doesn't employ traditional rhyme schemes. Rather, Chaplin invents form to suit her material. This freedom spells doom for most (and lesser) poets. It can only be handled with proper self-discipline, calling to mind the comment of French poet and critic Andre Gide: "Art is borne of constraint and dies from too much freedom."

One of the toughest jobs in editing poetry is that every mark on the page must be weighed. End punctuation, for example, has bipolar meanings in poetry and prose. In prose, punctuation brings before an editor relatively simple mechanical considerations. Does a period belong here? Is a comma missing or should one be removed? In poetry, every period, comma, semicolon, em dash, question mark, exclamation point (few if any!); every line break, which is itself a form of punctuation; every extra or missing space; line length; stanzas; the metrics or musicality of the words; and whatever else a poet might do ... all must contribute to the conveyance of meaning.

It's disappointing to see how many would-be "poets" employ these elements and marks carelessly and in a non-thinking manner. After having read a poem for enjoyment and then needing to provide a critique, I first examine the poem's arrangement on the page, especially the spacing and the punctuation. Are they strategic? Is there a reason for breaking the line where it breaks? Why is there an initial cap on this line but not on that? Why does a particular word constitute its own line? These must be deliberate and not random choices else you're dealing with a dabbler and not a poet.

I can attest to the reason for every mark in this book. If I couldn't find the reason, I made a change or invented one. Readers may agree or disagree with my editorial judgments, but rest assured: everything on the page in *Vertically Coastal* has a reason for being there (except, of course, any stray typos that escaped the kind and scrupulous attention of our army of proof readers).

Finally, let me share another tip not only for reading *Vertically Coastal* but any poetry. Slow down. Don't attack a poem. Approach it. Don't skim. Linger. Take each individual poem for itself, self-contained. Incorporate the full poetic context. Don't pick and choose this and that. For this collection, let each poem then build to something larger.

As Robert Scholes advises in his classic, *Elements of Poetry*, "We do not judge a poem by words or ideas taken out of context. We do not consider a statement in a poem without attention to its dramatic context, the overtones generated by its metaphors and ironies, the mood established by its metrics. And we try to give each element of every poem its proper weight."

From Scholes, we take his five suggestions intended to give the reader a "flexible procedure" he or she can employ in reading and understanding any poem.

1. "Try to grasp the expressive dimension of the poem first." Try to get a sense of what's going on at the literal level. For instance, I often try to restate the meaning of a poem in straight prose, summing up in as few words as I can what I think it means, as simply as possible. As Scholes advises, try to get "a clear sense of the nature and the situation of the speaker."

2. "Consider the relative importance of the narrative-dramatic dimension and the descriptive-meditative dimension." That's a fancy way of saying: Take a look at the "action" of the poem. What's going on? What's the writer trying to describe and via what objects, people, or situations?

3. "Re-read [the poem] with particular attention to the play of language." Readers most often skip this step. Any poem must be read at least twice to give it a fair chance with the reader. Word play, wit, metaphor, irony, images, and ideas "fit together and reinforce one another." "Play" — isn't that perfect?

4. "Re-read the poem yet again with special attention to its musical dimension." Focus on the cadence of the lines. Doing this places a figurative stethoscope to the poem's heart. You will hear the beat.

5. [R]eading the poem aloud can be helpful in establishing emphases and locating problems. Reading the poem out loud is a "final check" on our understanding of what it's trying to say. In reading poetry, and certainly in editing the poems of *Vertically Coastal*, I employ this "final check." If a section of the poem gives me problems, I can usually diagnose the situation after I read it out loud. My words will hear what my eye can't find.

Dear reader, I thank you for taking time with *Vertically Coastal.* Let me share one last piece of wisdom:

> *People possess four things*
> *that are no good at sea:*
> *anchor, rudder, oars,*
> *and the fear of going down.*
> — Antonio Machado,
> translated by Robert Bly

Do not fear sinking. Take Jerri Chaplin's hand as she walks you on the water.

— DAN VALENTI,
Stockbridge, Mass.

PART ONE

Charleston,
South Carolina

Charlie at the Carriage

The 2000-pound horse cannot lie long
in the street,
wounded, sleeping, or faking to play hooky
from pulling a period carriage.

Its ambitious weight will
crush its own organs — large, meaty, fragile
as red internal flowers —
in a silent, unconscious suicide, cannibalism without teeth,
dying, dumb, and unknowing.

Collapsing on a Charleston street on Christmas Eve,
Charlie does not know he will soon hoof into peace
without even moving a muscle, without a thought of
mare-mother, bluegrass field, or perplexed passenger;
without noticing he cannot feel the breath of the guide's words
floating like a cloud over the back of his head or wondering
why his eye is aligned with a blue-gray cobblestone
the color of a December Friday sky.

South Carolina Connections

I've got ancestors from upstate;
the Piedmont, the hills.
I've got ancestors from the Lowcountry,
flatlands on the ocean.
South Carolina has all the topography,
all the geography you'd study in a class.
Small towns strung together by country roads
snaking through places named Denmark and Florence.
Small towns hitch on to another
to make enough kids to need a school.
The towns run by the loyalty of who-you-know:
the good ol' boys, the former brothers-in-law of sorority sisters,
which church you attend, shared family Civil War stories,
beach houses, river trips with hounds on board.
Pat Conroy, patron saint.
The alumni of Clemson can do without the USC gang,
but after battles on the football field, they'll hug at family reunions
and go on dove shoots together.
Everyone sits on someone's piazza, drinking sweet tea,
sharing stories about those they love and hate,
often the same person.

Book Signing

In a Charleston studio,
the pen went incontinent
leaking on the letter "P."
I had long ago
surrendered the notion
my book would be perfect
but never suspected my
signature would mix inky
sludge and smudge,
a blur before
clean lines of poetry,
a trip-up before
an entrance
to dance.

Weathering

No matter how slow the birthing,
they burst out a squall or
burp little thunderrrrrumbles,
knee-over-shoulder tumbles
("emerge" — too elegant a word for how
they enter this world).
They arrive
an explosion of rain
and thick, foggy fluids,
tornado of textures,
smiling, raging sunburst
of small son.

They harbor in their tiny folded fists
hurricanes named after the alphabet
unleashed when their hands pop open,
fingers gardening into this new air, this new place,
home.

It begins one day
after which you are never the same
and to make a long story
— say 13 years plus —
short,
life with them is a silken siege of cycles:
sun and storm
twisters and blessed calm
balmy and bad
and back again.

Slowly, suddenly one day
they face the horizon
and move across a magic, invisible line.
The earth quakes a little then
and we stand, solid and shivery,
as we watch them, innocent,
walk into weather.

Slow Thursday
(for Peter)

Everything runs slow in the South;
the snow due at five falls at eleven.

The olive oil taste in the sourdough bread
kicks in halfway through the bitten slice.

We climb into bed at ten in the morning
after oatmeal and coffee, toast and tea
trading slow, sleepy kisses even after sleep,
limbs avalanching each into the other's
and finding in one another
the secret hidden places
snow can't freeze and sun can't melt.

The Official Language

Charleston does not speak with a Southern drawl.
Gullah's what you hear.
Gullah says, "Close de doe befoe you wash de flow."
and "Pleese lock de geyt befoe you leave laytah."
It calls our city "Chaa'ston" and peanuts "goobers."
Some think they're hearing a foreign language,
this English topped with Creole and African tribal words.
It's Porgy-perfect and Bess-beautiful
and, like sesame seeds,
something wonderful brought to us on slave ships.

NOTE: Gullah was made an official language in 1939.

The Official Color

The War of Northern Aggression
left Charleston in crumbling shape.
The North donated gallons of black paint,
but no local would use Yankee anything.
Mixing two parts Yankee black
with one part Rebel yellow
made a handsome, dark color
named Charleston Green.
It's our city's signature color
on benches, joggling boards, and shutters
bordering two sides of a window —
latched salvation, we hope,
if a hurricane happens.

Autumn Choice

This season
I choose to be an urban hermit,
stand in the dripping wax leaves of the
dormant grapevine planted in honor
of the son I love, and bury my face
in the fur of my four-legged, almond-eyed soulmate.

This season
I choose to sit in the tweedy lap of
my reading room chair
to take in the poetry of nature, the aroma of words,
cook five kinds of beans in my plugged-in pot,
five kinds of grain on my glowing stove.

This season
I choose to sit in the stillness of self,
to be like Emily Dickinson,
who sent downstairs this message to callers:
"I come down only for emergencies."

Sage
(for Peter)

Winter waits with me in the house we painted
warm and sage. Across town, you cook
for doctors and their slack-jawed dogs.
I rest deep in an old green chair
reading T.S. Eliot in hardback,
thinking of Williams,
eating a plum, proudly purple as a bruise
on the outside,
fibrous sage on the inside,
and heavy glossy heavy.
When you come home, you smell of garlic
and cold February air in a short year.
You lean your head into my sweatshirted chest.
I search your hair for a sprig of sage.

Tabled

Jessie was a nanny
who lived past 90.
She tied silk ribbons into the flaxen hair of the girl,
lovingly pulled the holes over the polished buttons
on the boy's navy blazer.
Every day at the park on the Battery
with a sharp view of Fort Sumter,
she boasted to the other help
about the meals she'd cook that week —
cheese grits and ham, shad roe, fried green
tomatoes, Carolina gold (a precious cargo of rice),
catfish, fried chicken, macaroni and cheese,
collards, black eyed peas and cow peas,
Frogmore Stew, corn bread and biscuits,
Coca Cola cake, and pecan pie —
year after year
until she died.

The children grew up and dined at Perdita's and Henry's,
but they never found a menu memory
as savory as Jessie's she-crab soup
or one as sweet as her old-time banana pudding.
Never.

Fruitful

All summer our grapes grow in heat down South.
Glossy purple/black, thick skin covers a pale-green innard,
as many seeds as birds swooping down to steal the fruit.
We never see those clusters, but in July in Massachusetts,
we grow perfect raspberries.
The day will come when we must stay in Charleston all year,
missing New England in the summer.
Then we will have our grapes, popping them into our
mouths, each a Massachusetts memory.
I'll bake a grape pie
just to help me stay different the way
the Berkshires do.

Papaya and Pomegranate

Touching on my marble kitchen counter
the yin and yang of fruits
the golden papaya and the dark red pomegranate.
Slice the papaya and empty its black seeds
leaving a smooth, perfect cavity.
The Pomegranate bursts its seeds out
like a farmer tossing beginnings into a field.
There is so much mystery and entanglement
in the pomegranate and such elegant grace
in the papaya.
But there can be no pairing.
A marriage would be difficult with one partner
so strong, streaming Biblical rubies.
In mating, he could strangle her
with those long, fibrous red ropes.
The yin and yang of fruits,
the Montagues and Capulets of the kitchen.

Salt

I'm resting
on the salt marsh
of my polished hardwood floor,
arms and legs outstretched —
floating in peace.
My lifeguards:
saltwater
sweat
tears —
have saved me from sinking,
from drowning.
They keep me not exactly upright
but uplifted just enough.

Molly and Netty

Molly Geller,
sweet, sturdy doorstop of a dog:
We competed for snacks
used the same eye drops
and relaxed into belly rubs.
Her death teased out an infant memory
of my grandparents' house, Augusta Road,
Greenville, South Carolina.
They had a black, iron-dog doorstop,
maybe a pug like Molly.
My grandmother, Netty, scared me by
talking to invisible people,
by saying "leave me alone" or "get away"
all the while shooing nonexistent flies
off her body.
Was she talking to me?
Her steely hair coiled like cinnamon buns,
one over each ear.
Her smile was yellow.
She was kind to me.
My mentor figured it out: Netty had schizophrenia and
told me never to call patients "schizophrenics."
A few years before he died, my father told me
he remembered as a boy
riding in a black car with his father
taking his mother to the mental hospital.
In and out
up and down
forward and back.

Even the adults did not know
which jumbled wires were doing what to her mind,
a frenzied brain dance with static steps, hissing like a broken TV.
I like it when tormented people die.
Death brings a quiet end to torture,
a much-needed rest.
Netty is buried with her
husband and parents, peaceful in a Greenville cemetery
with the kingly name
Graceland.

Snow Day

Charleston,
Arctic on the Atlantic,
38 the high today.
Last year we had a day's worth
of short, small snow.
My baffled dog, snow-virgin,
gingerly foot-printed her paws in it
then ate some,
Sno-cone on the backyard steps.

My Sick Sheltie

The first time in her six years
she's been sick.
The meds make her hungry.
She roams our house
licking the walls,
lumbers into the kitchen
to lick the 'fridge.
It's painful to watch.
The plastic heart protecting my real one
cracks into brittle red pieces
like the coating of a candy apple
or a shouting-STOP brake light.
It reassembles,
its magnetized pieces aping
a Saturday morning cartoon
where violence never leads to death.
The bling on her collar
jingles a St. Francis medal,
the closest she has to a cell phone.
I hope he hears and remembers
he's on eternal call.

Nightmare Chair

My son's nightmares scared his hair
into electric stars and angry arcs.
Fearscapes filled his head, and he fled on bare feet
to my room, to my husbandless, fatherless bed.

Me, same age, same stage, 1954.
The chair was a huge, grey elephant peering from the left
into your bed, cradling me from hours of
terrified thinking and night noises.
O, mighty hunter! Safari screams and marriage dreams.
Built to bear burdens, there was no delicacy about it.
Reliable, trustworthy, solid shelter to the sole, fearful child.
Recovered, stabbed, smiled upon, recovering.
Starstruck, scarred, sun-splashed on a Honolulu lanai,
home again to Charleston, arms open.

Manicured

Porcelain petite
Vietnamese young girl —
The picture we like to frame
of the hard-working immigrant —
dons a white paper mask
like an ER surgeon
and paints blue-black dolphins
on the acrylic nails of a brown woman.
The dolphins will jump
toward the pool of a computer screen
or curl, hidden, in the hands of small children.
Ten click-clacking small spears
of art and artifice wave
into the humid, holiday air,
July Fourth in South Carolina.
"Gotta take those into the Atlantic
now," I say, warily white.
"Into the Atlantic, off Charleston."
If the nails were brown and the woman
blue-black, would there be more wails
than dolphins, more singin' the blues?

Oh, say can you see, and do you not
remember Bob Dylan groaning,
"I pity the poor immigrant"?

Carolina Kayaking

A swarm of shrimp
bubble the river top
in silence but for robinsong and grackletail.
Wild rice grows thick as corn stalks, wind sliding
through slim green lines reaching toward a perfect blue sky.
We are nourished by even the hint of a crop, by the knowledge that
hidden from our daily city, the plants grow here, tender and tall.
The symphony starts in the mud, a quiet opus of heartbeats.

A mullet jumps flapsmacking the air of June's last day,
pushing with gills and tail the resistance of sticky summer air
moving lazily into July, Gershwinesque.

Between river and creek,
our paddles learn their rhythm:
dip, pull, glide, a twist on the right
a shift to the left
aiming for one choreographed, effortless motion,
a silken machine,
a laughing salute to the vulture circling overhead,
to the place where every living thing knows,
grows, yields, melds, and stands alone.

Shrimping

These boats are linked to the land.
The 4 a.m. men drive them, trailing
like history, like missions, like need,
to the dark Wadmalaw waters
pinpoint-lit with the
shining September eyes of
shrimp swimming silver.

The Space Between

The space between rice field and crop,
crop to freedom,
is the darkest price.

"black bird singing in the dead of night ..."

The space between each drumbeat footstep of dance
is an imaginary chain
to be broken, loose as leaves.

The space between wings is bone and body
body, soul, and power.

The space between words is the syntax of silence.

The space between animal sounds is the ancient story
between reedy grasses, air alive with the
buzzwhiz of insects. A droning, some days.

The space between one tree and its reflection
is the mind's mirror,
between the burst of orange and the leafy green,
the bright imagined color.

The space between stillness and nature's symphony
is marsh music,
a crescendo of Carolina breeze.

The space between wingtip and cloud

is feathered strength:
confidence, clarity, and hope.

"take these broken wings ..."

Between the quiet and birdsong
is joy building
"learn to fly ..."
soaring in Carolina sky.

Dialogues

#1 OL' TIME RELIGION

No skyscrapers pierce the Charleston skyline,
only 167 steeples in the Holy City on the Peninsula.
Newcomers are asked where they go to church
before they're asked their names.
Restless and helpless after 9-11,
I wanted to bake cookies for my neighborhood firemen.
They work in an 1887 station built for horse-drawn engines,
its floor grooved for hoof traction.
Now the engine is custom built to fit under low arches.
In the grocery, my sweet ingredients lined the slow-moving belt.
"Look like you bakin' a dessert," said the hunched
old lady behind me.
"Yes'm, cookies for my firemen."
"Well, you are a fine Christian lady," she smiled.
"Actually, I'm Jewish," I had to say.
"Oh my. Well, that's okay. The Old Testament's good, too."

#2 I.D. ME

My husband and I stood in line to vote.
He told the elderly lady handling paper work,
"My wife's right behind me."
She looked at my driver's license as if I were ET.
"How long have you been married?" she asked.
How dear! She must think we are newlyweds.
"Ten years," I smiled, thinking our love must radiate.

She snapped, "You can't vote. You have to change your name
within three months after getting married."
Quietly, I explained I had not changed my name.
Her mouth puckered prissy.
"You a doctor or lawyer or somethin'?" she asked.
I could feel my husband, the Brooklyn bulldog,
about to shout at the frail, white-haired
lady;
I muzzled his arm.
"No," I said, sweet as sugar.
"I'm just a married woman who kept her own name."
She sniffed and let me pass
to exercise my right to vote
on yet another choice.

Report From Hollywood, S.C.

Dateline — HOLLYWOOD, S.C. Nov. 25 —
The 40-year-old broke up
with his girlfriend
only to awaken this
morning to find his car
covered in grits.
Grits like buttered snow, poured all over
the roof, hood, and trunk.
He figured it was the ex, alright,
harassing him in Hollywood.
The sheriff warned she's on notice
for trespassing
and told the guy to get the car cleaned.
I'd say:
Call all your friends with forks.

Southern Sunday Morning
Weather Forecast

Bill, Tom, and Rob,
our meteorological stars,
are dark on Saturday nights.
The new guys, personable and peppy,
pull that particular shift.
It's the same on every channel:
"When you head out to church Sunday morning,
your weather will be ... "
No complaint changes the commentary.
If I don't head out to church,
will I have completely different weather?
What if I am Muslim, Jewish, Hindu, Buddhist, or,
God forbid, an atheist?
Will I get hailstones and lightning instead of
cottony clouds and clear blue skies?
Maybe the winds will change when the sun
ceases to shine on the Confederate flag
still flying on the grounds of the State Capitol.

Re-enactment

November 14, 2010,
the Battle of Secessionville
is re-enacted for the 20th time
at Boone Hall Plantation
(two for one gander at the Shames of the South).
The players (soldiers) arrive in their costumes (uniforms)
to play out the June 1862 battle with their
children saluting and their women watching,
praying not to be widowed.
That mid-June day, the Confederate troops
pushed back the Union on James Island
where even today Yankees aren't a ball team.
Should some of the losing battles be re-created
to see if the outcome changes, if in 1865,
the South retroactively wins the "War of Northern Aggression"?

Snowed-in Sunday

Spring's second day.
The plane home folds its wings
like origami
under the weight of snow,
crosses its chest in the stance of
no negotiation.

We are still young enough
to appreciate the unexpected,
to savor being snowed in
on a Sunday in a hotel bed
in Manhattan. Outside, the
paper-weight Christmas scene
belies Spring. The calendar says
"yes," but the runway runs nowhere.

Down home, you are a Yankee on eternal probation.
Here, the Southern gentleman, venturing into the freeze
returning with a barricade of bagels, hot coffee, and the Sunday slab
of "All The News That's Fit To Print."

Later, we'll go to the Cineplex, bury our faces
in troughs of hot popcorn, and read subtitles.
Now we re-read the old comforting news of each other's bodies,
spontaneous in this snow-created hiatus between
holiday and home.
You indulge me in telling Saturday's dream:
boys back to babies, curly-haired, heavy and sweet with sleep,
one leaning on my shoulder, one with his head in my lap.

The lap of someone 32 not 50.
Who I was …
who they were …
thawed out by the snow
in dreamy display.

Birthday Joyride

The day my baby turned 18,
he was thousands of miles away
surfing the Pacific
but on my mind
all the time.

As it happened, I drove that day
to the next-door state of Georgia,
a joy ride with Paul in search of
a Japanese tattoo of tranquility,
surfing the Savannah Highway away
from South Carolina where permanent,
inky decoration of the body is so
offensive as to be illegal.

Paul said he would buy me my own tattoo,
a mark of truth or tawdriness.

But my husband said if I got one,
don't bother to come home.
Ah, that was tempting alright.

In the tattoo parlor, the violent pictures
threw me, and the single teenagers with their babies,
and the price list for piercing of body parts
I never knew existed.
I bet my baby didn't even surf by them
in the birth canal 18 years ago today.
And now he is surfing clean in a churn
of blue wave out West.

I got a fake tattoo in Japanese and colors.
It painted my bicep like a bruised oyster
bursting from a shell, and I realized
one day that bicep and the inky Japanese symbol
would shrivel like a dried-out Georgia peach,
like summer flowers in South Carolina,
like a baby going prune-y in the Pacific,
surfing, surfing till the brilliant sunset
tattooed on the California sky
washes over his special day.

NOTE: Tatooing is now legal in South Carolina

Birds

*(for Moore, a friend who recently lost her father.
I had no idea he had been a builder of birdhouses.)*

Tender raven-haired bird,
you nurture your broken wing
hoping it will heal.

I have perched on the same branch of pain,
wrapping my claws around it, digging in,
holding on for dear life.

Sometimes I fell, losing my balance,
a mynah drunk on mango wine,
a wrong-footed flamingo.
Sometimes I could open my mouth and sputter
something akin to a mix of prayer and birdsong.

I believe you will believe me:
On what would have been his 90th birthday,
my father appeared in the brightest red
and sat on the edge of the birdbath.
"Heaven must be a heck of a place," I cracked.
"You go up a Jew and come back a Cardinal."
He flipped into the water, flapped his wings
to wash his body, dipped his head, and
flew up to a bough to sun-dry.

He comes often and stays long,
usually when I need him most.

Your wing will heal.
Your heart will soften with a lining of feathers
and become both
high-flying and grounded.

Colonial Lake, Charleston
(a poem for children)

On its surface, fish do flip
(have you ever wondered if a fish can slip?)
Hopeful fishermen angle for dinner.
If they're unlucky, they might grow thinner.

And I wonder, child, have you heard
the sound of a plopping, bellyflopping bird?
Pelicans fall kerplunk in this lake.
It's a very good thing a lake can't break.

There's action on the outside, it's true,
with roller bladers skating in twos,
bikers on their cycling wheels,
dogs of all sizes sniffing for meals,
joggers running for miles and miles
(why is it joggers rarely smile?).

You're invited any day
to see Colonial Lake at play!

84, 82

At 84,
my father bought a BMW
the price of a small house
somewhere South.

A travel tank, interiors
trimmed with tortoise
shell, like so many broken
eyeglass frames — recycled,
lined up, and pieced.

At 82
and shrinking, my mother
does not need all the leg room
the Bavarians provided, and so
the floor of the passenger side
unsullied and deeply carpeted
holds her outstretched cane.

At 84 and 82, they drive to
the country club
for lunch,
where she cannot tolerate most
of the food and he cannot remember
the number that makes him a member.

The fingers that typed editorials
that changed the world
shake

and food falls between them
like feathers down a street grate,
like opportunities to love falling
through the cracks.

She frowns, sometimes snaps,
as head lowered, he looks to his lap.

At 84 and 82 they drive to sunshine
movies where they still delight in
getting their senior discount, not quite
believing a small cut of good fortune.

When the daughter inquires, he says
the sound was too soft.
She says in a voice far softer
than cinema audio could ever be,
"I was confused."

Burial of a Friendship

Imagined, a Southern cemetery
heavy with magnolias and mourning,
warm words, full heart, elegant epitaph,
celebratory memories and fondly recalled affection
or
the fiery consummation of cremation,
the cool, soft beauty of ashes countering the flame,
distillation to the purest form, the foundation of
solid bone shifted to grey memory, an urn, a shrine,
something beautiful to hold, somewhere holy to visit.

Reality: a pauper's grave,
stained sheet of a shroud encumbering
the tossed-in Mozart or eternally lonely
Person X.

Swamp Angels, Hill Women

Graveyard, Church on the Hill, Lenox, Mass.,
Fanny Kemble, English actress

I had a mutual love affair with Lenox, Massachusetts,
a place where I performed Shakespeare.
When I newly married the American,
Pierce Butler, we came to Lenox in style, driving four horses.
He then inherited the largest plantation in Georgia.
Shocked by the conditions and treatment of slaves,
I withstood it as long as I could.
We divorced in 1849.
I bought a Lenox house, The Perch,
two miles west of Hawthorne's red house.
Peaceful summers, 1836-1853. I was friends
with the literati, abolitionists in the Berkshires
and Boston, with all manner of delightful people.
I loved the Berkshire scenery.
I gave Lenox the clock in the tower
at the Congregational Church on the Hill.
I said, "I will not rise to trouble anyone
if they will let me sleep there.
I will only ask to be permitted once in a while
to raise my head and look out over the glorious scene."
Not to be ... I rest in London.
I wrote an antislavery book, I acted, I traveled,
I enjoyed my friends.
I never remarried.

Annie Shaw, widow of Col. Robert Gould Shaw

Unlike the actress Miss Kemble, I was a private person.
I would never ask to lift my head again to see Lenox.
Better I simply remain at rest; my eyes would not see
but no one would glimpse me, either.
My privacy demanded I tell my husband to burn my letters
when he went to war in South Carolina.
Foolish: What had I to say that called for burning?
Thankfully, his letters remained to tell the story of his 54th regiment,
 1,100 black men led by 37 white officers led by my husband,
Col. Robert Gould Shaw, age 25, invited to the job
by Gov. John Andrews himself.
394 black men from Massachusetts,
runaway slaves from South Carolina and other points South,
recruits from Canada, New York State, mid-western states.
No one thought they'd be good fighters.
Rob grew up in an abolitionist family in Boston
as I did in New York and Lenox.
After two years of courtship, despite his mother's dismay,
we married in 1863.
She thought marrying me would distract him from war duties.
We knew marrying would bring him serenity.
There was no more beautiful place to honeymoon
than Lenox's Vent Fort, built by my father, Ogden Haggerty.
Our stay lasted a precious four days
before Rob was called to lead training near Boston.
Twenty-two days to teach everything
from weaponry to wearing shoes for the first time.

Ready for duty, they paraded down Boston streets on May 22, 1863.
We family stood on the balcony at 44 Beacon.
Rob saluted us, his sword to his lips.
His sister Ellen said,
"His face was the face of an angel, and I felt perfectly sure
he would never come back."
We had been married 26 days.
I never saw him again.
His letters, though, were numerous.
He learned white soldiers were paid $13 a month;
blacks, $10 with $3 deducted for the uniform.
Every one of his soldiers refused pay.
Rob did the same.
He journeyed to Washington to fight for equal pay,
which started after 18 months.
He didn't live to receive a paycheck
or see a black soldier receive his.
His black soldiers were cooks, chaplains, carpenters,
laborers, surgeons, and spies, all brave fighters.
Not one deserted.
They respected Rob as he did them,
always with an eye on equality,
fighting for their rights more than territory.
But territory had to be won to capture Charleston.
A returning reporter, Edward L. Pierce, gave me the account
of the assault on Fort Wagner, South Carolina.
Rob had entrusted letters and personal items to Pierce
to give to me "in case."
He sought me out.

Fort Wagner was sited on Morris Island.
At 7:45 pm, July 18, 1863, Rob told his men,
"I want you to prove yourselves.
The eyes of thousands will be on you tonight."
It did not surprise me that Rob ran down the beach
leading his regiment, the Atlantic on one side,
a creek on the other.
Waving his sword, he climbed the parapets
to the earthwork fort
inhabited by more Confederate men than expected.
He was shot in the heart, fell into the fort,
and died immediately.
The bearer of Old Glory went down, too,
but Sgt. William Carney grabbed the flag,
and it never touched the ground.
After the battle, with half our troops dead,
an officer requested the return of Rob's body.
He had been stripped to underwear
and carried around Fort Wagner.
Then, according to Confederate Brigadier General Johnson Hagood,
"We threw him in a ditch, buried him with his niggers."
This move to humiliate the Shaw family backfired.
My father-in-law spoke for us:
"We hold that a soldier's most appropriate burial place
is on the field where he has fallen."
Rob and his ditch-mates became Swamp Angels,
bathed repeatedly by the sea, holy water,
a rhythm and rite of purification, I believe.

I moved to Europe.
I heard the artist Saint-Gaudens created
a beautiful monument in Boston Common.
Humble as ever, Rob's father said he did not want
Rob portrayed atop a horse but as a foot soldier.
The artist disagreed and so did I.
He was the Colonel in command and should be seen as such.
In his 25 years, Rob accomplished everything he wanted
except to write poetry.
He wrote but one line.
I lived my last two years at Vent Fort.
I never remarried.

Epilogue:
In 1900, Sgt. William Carney was the first black man to be awarded
   the Congressional Medal of Honor for service in the Civil War.
In 2008, the 54th Regiment was reactivated as a
   Massachusetts National Guard Ceremonial Unit.
In 2011, a battle still rages at the privately owned Morris
   Island, this time over the building of houses.
No remnant of Fort Wagner remains. The
   Atlantic Ocean still watches.

Timing

Yes
there is global colding and
it has hit us to our own degree
in the South.
About February or March,
I start to visualize Berkshire lakes,
not as they are in those months
but as I love them in summer,
sun gleaming on smooth surfaces.
I keep my view superficial,
not looking below to weeds
or the truth of murky mud and mussels.
I imagine lakeside cabins opening
to breezes ruffling cotton curtains.
I daydream children swimming out to rafts
and a sun reluctant to let go of the sky-blue day.
I see walking along Stockbridge Bowl,
eating lobster on the deck of the pub on Pontoosuc,
taking the dog to Onota to rest on its slight slope.
My thoughts drift to smaller lakes and ponds,
to punctuations of the green countryside.
By May, cold is not the issue.
We feel the prospect of heat hovering over us,
the sea-smelling outstretched pelican wing.
Our hearts long for what we've not got here.
I whisper into Phoenix's velvet, cocked ear,
"It's time to go."

PART TWO

Here
to
There

Vertically Coastal

HERE
I live vertically coastal:
seven Southern months,
five in the North, inching toward five and a half.
Charleston's my birthright,
a generational birth at that,
in the "right" hospital to a family who arrived
in the 19th century.
A family full of cousins and rainclouds with
an infrastructure of lace.
Expectations, obligations, Southern secrets
(antique rugs covering years of swept-under truths).

My Lowcountry has sweeping salt marshes, the Cooper and
Ashley rivers forming the Atlantic, a wealth of waterways
reverberating with seabird calls:
ospreys, terns, gulls,
the ever-silent pelican.
Boats that see no need to go elsewhere.
There are mysteries tucked in the curls of
wrought iron gates, seagrass baskets woven
to hold stories, echoes of *Porgy and Bess*,
fences whose owners were "too poor to paint,
too proud to whitewash."
Their descendants cling to the war, but you can
peek at peace through the fences,
finding magnolias and camellias.

Nearby stand white-frosted confectionary mansions,
often father-daughter wedding gifts.
Charleston serves gumbo and red rice
with low-key gusto and hushed hospitality,
racks up media awards for manners, and is
too polite and dignified to boast.
Its charm is genuine, down to its unique accent
and rainbow-painted houses.
I walk its rose-grey cobblestone streets,
tricky alleys of get-away pirates, and
know of more characters than a convoy of
horse-drawn carriages could carry.

THERE

As soon as we cross the Castleton-on-Hudson Bridge,
my heart quickens,
turning me inside-out.
In the Berkshires
I stand grounded,
rooted primal,
like an ancient woodland tree.
The extraneous disappears.
The spiritual emerges.
I am pared to the core.

My animal spirit reawakens.
I am the fox, the bear,
the brown rabbit scampering in celebration,
my small heart pumping joy.

My backyard forest flings me free.
My home soil grows ripe fruit.
Far-going fields, mountains some call hills,
cool lakes and family farms
make my blood beat happy and slow.
I live in the beauty of Shaker ways.
I'm in dog clothes all day.
My friends know how to leave me alone.
I love to find tracks, animal or train.
I spot fast-moving trains from my window,
get to know a schedule I could forget
but for my pulse's anticipation.
Even the sounds of trains are theater, film, or book.
They take me on an adventure, making me more than I was.
I love the clack of trains on track
and the afterward echo of quiet.

All summer my body inhales dance,
my muscles remember
as I rest my head on Jacob's Pillow,
sanctuary where escaping slaves rode the
Underground Railroad.
I hear symphonies in the trees.

HERE & THERE

In Charleston, tree moss makes a canopy, a hiding
curtain of cool privacy. The Palmetto transports
me to Caribbean islands of trade, historic days.
Here, the past reigns.

Up North, in autumn, my maple wears a skirt
of burnished, fallen leaves
swirl-dancing at her base.
Someone always asks the unanswerable:
where's home?

PART THREE

Pittsfield,
Massachusetts
& The Berkshires

Berkshire Barns

Berkshire barns
die beautifully, their history deep
in the wood,
their stories wind-told
through cracks.
The faint aroma of hay
remains.
There may be a ghost of
a goat
or a sole hen feather
the weather
has not stolen.
Mostly they stand empty,
wither, and sag,
with no protective farmer
to say thank you and goodbye.
They have the longest of natural deaths,
the most profound of green burials.

Dogs Seeing

The stones say something.
My dog's nose picks up the words.
She can hear, too, meaning in the moaning wind
and the movements on Onota Lake.
She cannot speak to me but
we have conversations.
When she presses her body parallel to my legs
in the sunrise bed,
I like to believe that means "I love you,"
but what do I know?
If dogs think in pictures,
what slide show is playing now?
Is she seeing back to the Shetlands
where the sheep, ponies, and dogs were small,
the better to dwell on space-deprived islands?
Does she glimpse a swatch of tartan
or an ancestor herding?
Does the Greyhound see the replay of his last race
or the Canaan dog look back to Israel
and wonder what went so terribly wrong?

Country School Busses

On the Berkshires' rural roads after Labor Day,
you see the school busses
downloading kids in the afternoon.
Grandparents wait to welcome them, not protect them.
The kids are taught not every adult is to be feared.
In the country, kids still walk home,
their parents are working not worrying.
Brothers and sisters play-fight
kids talk to neighbors,
ask the elderly how they're doing
stop, say hello,
take a quick run with a frisky dog,
pause to give a horse
lunch's leftover apple.
The scene's even sweeter if there are
crunchy leaves to scuffle through.
Later at home, they reconnect with their families
and cell phones.
But for a few soft moments
in the afternoon,
they are disconnected from the school day,
from their machines,
and — just by walking home —
repeat a bit of heritage and history.

Magic Karma Pants

His kaleidoscope tie-dyed pants
were a tent, a parachute, a large place with legs.
Did they power the leaps that almost kicked gravity
on its ass?
Did they create the quick turns spitting sweat from his
electric curls onto the studio walls at Kripalu?
They came from a no-website stall in Mumbai,
he panted, breathless when I caught him after class.
"I'm very attached to them."
He bit his lip in thought.
"Very, very attached to them. Because I am so
attached, I must part with them."
An evolved soul, a Zen moment.

    For me, a prophet.
    For him, a profit.

Sister Cecilia

Never having met,
we arranged to in the café at Kripalu.

I e-mailed: "I'll be wearing dark glasses."
You fired back:
"I'll be the one in the habit."

But you weren't.
You were dressed as the yoga student, yoga teacher:
A longish black dress with sleeves to the wrist.
a head wrap resembling gauze,
little froggy foot gloves
with a separate place for each toe.

You tell travel tales to one who imagines
cloistering walls almost always say no
and speak more of prison than Paradise.
You bend into yoga as easily as you kneel.

People assume you are impoverished
when, in fact, your life is rich with freedom.
You move and learn,
a sisterhood awaiting your return.
Your slim gold wedding band gleams.
You have found the joy and serenity
we all pray for in marriage,
in life.

Person Eats Person

The writer's beautiful, beloved dog,
the one that changed his life,
out of the blue began to bite.
There were several victims — some, children.
His choice was spend thousands on a brain scan
or put the dog to sleep.
He carried the dog's large, limp body up a Berkshire hill
too steep for his health,
buried him, and stayed quiet there
in a reverence of gratitude.

Outraged fans phoned and emailed
asking how he could kill this magnificent
animal.
They stopped short of performing
a resurrection rite at the burial spot on the farm.

At a reading, a stooped man stood and said softly
"I've lost a dog. I've lost a child. I can tell you,
there's no comparison."

Alarm
(September 11, 2006)

A crisp apple of a Fall day;
the neighborhood dogs bite in at six a.m.
barking an alarm to an unseen sun.

Baby, Riley, Pippin, Sophie, Phoenix:
four-legged alarms,
voices jousting through open windows,
short curtains ruffling in the breeze
on another beautiful September day.

Who wants to get up out of beds of certainty,
warm covers pulled to our chins or even over our heads,
feet held fast by the belly of a warm dog bound in
love and loyalty?
Who wants to let go the hand of the sideways spouse?
Who wants to swing the legs over the side
and touch the cold floor of a new day?

The clock replaces the dogs alerting alarm
and suddenly, it's as if the whole room goes red.
Fingers touch the sound down to calm.

Today the explosion is of leaves:
amber, orange, crimson
falling from the wet, the cool,
the green safe places where nothing burns.

J.T.

My Berkshire neighbor doesn't know
I spied on him on his Hawaiian honeymoon.
Waiting for a bus in Waikiki,
I hid behind a palm tree once I spotted them,
impossibly lanky and beautiful,
cavorting on the beach at the Moana Hotel.
If anyone recognized them, they didn't let on.

Every ocean wave was a set of lyrics washing over me,
disbelieving this god and goddess
romping before my widened fan eyes.
Carly wore a black bikini, legs up to her wild hair.
James was the LP picture with which I'd fallen in love —
Soulful eyes, sensitive face, poet and troubadour.
I let the bus roll by more than once.

They have long been sand-blown apart.
But he has settled beautifully into age
in the Berkshires, singing his wisdom and gentle kindness,
at home at Tanglewood and the Colonial,
generous beyond score, when all he needs to do
is sing "Stockbridge to Boston"
until his country road runs out.

Practice

In the Berkshires, if you're lucky,
you live next to a musician practicing.
Some summers, we lived near
Symphony players
festooning our trees with notes blown
into the outside world through an open window.
Light breezes blew them criss-crossing the boughs,
and there was music in the air
somersaulting symphonies
all afternoon.
More than concerts,
I love hearing
the tune ups, the warm ups,
the ups and downs of practice
on a sunny day
in my raspberry-growing
Berkshire backyard,
where the notes are just
passing through.

Pay Attention

Cousin,
why do you check your mind at the door?
Why hang it on the hat rack like
a woolen cap
motorcycle helmet
(or bike or football)
Indian headdress
yarmulke
hajib
ear muffs
bonnet
designer hat
scarf a la Jackie or Marilyn?
Please, before we talk,
before you pretend to listen
or we ascend into argument,
get your mind clicked into place.
Collect your head covering on the way out.

Bones

In the New Mexico desert,
sun-bleached bones, cow skulls, dried limbs strewn
among the cactus thorns, green but thirsty still,
wet within
thick, plant bodies yearning to be slit, to leak into the bones.
Lightyears away, lightmiles
in a Massachusetts bed,
the bones of a woman's hips
skim the Atlantic, inviting the ocean to hear,
asking the waves to fill the void of the
desert cow-skull cavity.

Hubris

I have front-to-back bears.
My back screen door to the forest,
my red front door to Jason Street.
I am the bear.
I know how to negotiate the forest
lumbering high, squatting low.
I know the garbage cans on the front lawn
serve gourmet leftovers from a pro chef, Tuesdays.
He owns a small dog I could savage
for dessert.
I know no one pauses at the stop sign.
I'm always free to flee.
To say I am the bear reveals
I'm not the bear at all.

Adopting Apples

When it's Fall enough
I go to the orchard.
I will not pick in August,
no earlier than late September
sliding into October.

The rows of trees make avenues —
new paths to walk, treasure trails to tread,
architected with integrity, taking me to
American places with myriad names.

Every year I swear I'll remember them.
Every year I forget.

The orchard is natural but not wild, not overgrown
with witchy excess, with the darkness of nature
obscuring harmony. No gnarled roots will trip you
or wayward tree arm strike you.
Humanity is nature's offshoot and every season
I stretch taller, grow out of my ribs
in a treelike way I believe impossible.
I aim for the highest apple on the tree.
I reach a fingertip closer to the cloudless sanctuary sky,
drape my hand, and cover an apple with that crowning grasp.
The apple rests, ripening on its birth bough till I gently pull.
I hold it as I bow to it, a Namaste,
grateful it is now my adopted red.

Shining, it is happy to be chosen,
to travel,
to do its work unquestioning,
to know within hours
it will become a dancer,
a mother,
a writer of poems.

Silly Apple Agenda

Jonagold, Macintosh,
Northern Spy,
living in Cortland, Rome, or another Empire.
Hanging out with green accomplice, Granny Smith.
I'll write a mystery about him
or knife him to eat with cheese.

Past Paper

As close to the rivers as waterfowl,
the broken-windowed paper mills
have time on their hands and no morning whistle
to rouse them to action.
They sit and open a brick eye to remember
the angels in the architecture,
the dignity of details in design, the pestle and the pulp.
They are empty museums, bereft of workers and product,
people and paper.
These were palaces of industrial architecture
providing drafting paper for big plans,
paper collars for the well-dressed man,
stock certificates imprinted with anticipation,
stationery made from cotton.
A regret to a tea,
condolences to a new widow,
an angry letter to a lawyer,
a young man's first love letter.
Sixty-five of them in the 19th century,
Berkshire bustling, busy by day,
quiet, cozy with the water at restful night.
How I would have loved to have been a curator of paper.

Mail At The Mount

Edith Wharton's breakfast tray
was brought to her in bed,
holding her meal and mail.
I long for the time when mail was delivered
more than once a day
brought up on a silver tray.
I'd love to write with a quill dipped in indigo ink.
Now I am used to finding a mailbox
full of dried leaves in Autumn,
a container of humid air in Summer,
a petrified palmetto bug in Winter —
not petrified-terrified but an amber,
crackly and dry, whiskey-colored frozen roach.
In Spring, bits of magnolia blossom and pollen.
Bills, however, drop in regularly.
I e-mail to live a modern life, though e-mail's been displaced.
I climb into the cell for emergencies.
Text is not instant for me and does not require another human.
My face will be on a book when I've earned it,
and I think only birds should twitter.
Yes, I'm a dino with an empty mailbox.
I mourn what I understand and what I don't.
I mourn what we've lost.

Dreaming of the Pillow

I started ballet at four,
my curtained shower a huge rectangular stage.
I studied with Miss Minette Starts, New Orleans, La.,
with my friends of apple-pie-'50s names:
Linda, Carol, Ellen, Susan, Barbara, Nancy.
Five years later, I *jetéd* across the Pacific and landed on Oahu.
I read everything I could on Jacob's Pillow.
Ted Shawn and Ruth St. Denis looked like Indians,
Isadora Duncan, Greek.
I asked my mother, "What's a Javanese dancer?"
"They must mean Japanese," she sniffed.
That was the 1950s in Hawaii, not yet a state,
a cut-off world unto itself.
Sitting on my island covered in gardenia, jasmine
and bougainvillea, Massachusetts seemed so *exotic.*
Underneath thin sheets, with a flashlight and
transistor tuned to KPOI, I figured one day
I could get to Boston but where the heck was Becket?
My girlish dream receded.
Many steps and turns later after years of jumps and falls,
my magic prince husband took me there
when life seemed freshly full of possibilities.
The mix of art, artifice, and nature was breathtaking.
I was home, my second Jerusalem.

Salvation
(for Rebecca)

I danced for you today.
The lift of my *relevé*
the slow bend of my *plié*
my arm's gentle arc
circling my head.

As all the dancers formed a
circle,
you were in the corner,
at an angle,
but a necessary part of the piece.
I danced for you today.
I could not dance without you.

To a Dancer, For New Year's

I may not know your name
but my finger brushes yours.
Our palms mirror the one, the other,
building bridges of sweat and silk.
My footprints fall on yours,
yours stand on mine,
gliding, jumping, stomping, swaying,
leaning, bending, leaving, staying.
Your jewel-box heart spills onto the floor
giving me emeralds of empathy, diamonds of daring.
We exchange bits of frayed ribbon and speckles of rust.
We give each other handfuls of trust.

I may not know your name
but feel your spirit in the steps,
your mettle in the music.
This year, all year,
dance me your story.

Birthright

(for Savion Glover's baby son)

We grow
in the tap-dance room
of our mother's womb.
Rhythm, the soft riveter,
marks the beat on our
burgeoning baby bones,
sloshing to our mom's music.

We're born dancing.

Here in the big green
beautiful bowl of the Berkshires
you've taken the stage at Jacob's Pillow
in your little orange suit
bopping the mic,
a squatter on your place in tap's line
in June sun,
one hand lifted and lilting,
reaching to your birthright.

Dying to Dance

My heart flies to her,
the rest of my body retreats.
To dance alongside her
feels like performing a death duet.
Her energy comes from being high on nothing.
The less she eats, the faster she twirls.
The higher she jumps, the happier she is.
So goes the power
of control's choreography.
At break, her smile is too big,
her conversation nonstop,
her manner pure manic.
If she's not a size zero already,
she's aiming for it.
Our adoring culture forgets
zero equals nothing.

Residential Reincarnation

Their days were spent in splendor in Boston and New York.
Summers, they wanted an inland Newport,
mountains to supplement their seaside resorts.
What industrialists want, they get.
Think Carnegie, think Westinghouse.

Even before the Civil War, construction started
and by 1890, the Gilded Age frosted the Berkshires
with glittering estates, golden homes their owners called Cottages.
Little get-aways with up to 100 rooms,
93 cottages jeweled the hills before 1900.

Their summer included sumptuous teas, lavish parties,
sporting events like golf and the game where
an innocent fox is hounded by hounds and horsemen.
Everything prepared, served, and swept up by servants.

Such fairy tale summers, starting with once upon a time,
losing the happily ever after.
In a Fall of Rome kind of way,
in an income tax and stock market crash kind of way,
the cottages loomed too large, lifestyles overly rich,
every house top heavy and falling on its side.
Reincarnation was ripe to arrive.

Highwood, which had served the Tappens well,
reappeared in 1937 as Tanglewood.
What if it had preferred to be a tangle of woods?
Did anyone ask Shadowbrook if it wanted to burn

and return as a Jesuit School?
John Sloane's home became Cranwell,
resort scene of a spa and carriage house burning.
The Choates did well by Naumkeag,
and Edith Wharton stayed at the Mount till 1910.
Maybe the Mount would have wished to lift its skirt and trot away.
Blantyre, Wheatleigh, the others: Did anyone give you a choice?
Ah, it is the same for people.
No one's asked me if I want to come back
as a butterfly, a fly, or butter.
The gods decide. It is ours to accept and make the best of,
just as Ventfort Hall may long to be Vent Fort,
with less foot traffic and more aristocratic footfalls.
Just for the record,
I'd like to be reborn a giraffe,
and not a gilded one.

The Prizes

I. EDITH

I loved to go to the theater at The Mount,
its corners crumbling, its wallpapers peeling
like sunburnt skin.
You could see Keanu Reeves dodging mosquitoes
in Shakespeare or Tina Packer in a teatime play,
tea and lemon cookies served with the seat.
Those cookies were madeleines evoking times past,
when Edith Wharton taste-made the world:
thoughts of horse-drawn carriages, English gardens,
leather libraries, the detailed pantry,
the bell system to ring for servants.
The Mount as designed by Edith in 1902,
the gardens, too.
In Edith's day, The Mount was perfection
fitting for the girl born Edith Jones in New York
as in "Keeping Up with the Joneses."
She, swaddled in elegance, swathed in it,
exuded it, never evaded it.
Living in grandeur and propriety,
she traveled to Europe.
Standing on the deck of the ship,
she stared into the portholes of the privileged,
the micro-world of her peers.
She retained what she liked, inhaled rarefied air,
and — to prick consciences and provoke consciousness —
wrote novels and stories, books biting wit and insight
into the upper classes, yappy books that would not go away.

In the Berkshires, she soiled her hands writing *Ethan Frome*.
She wrote about villas, gardens, design, and décor;
about class differences in New York and Europe,
where she had A-list literary and intellectual friends.
Proper and discreet, Edith started an affair in 1908
once the doctors declared her husband's depression incurable.
After the divorce she moved to France
and dirtied her hands again, performing charitable works
to support French Imperialism.
In Europe, she remained one of the literati
and returned only once to the U.S.,
to receive an honorary doctorate from Yale in 1923,
that on the heels of being the first woman
to win the Pulitzer Prize for Literature, 1921,
for *The Age of Innocence*.
She lived in a country place called *Saint-Brice-sous-Foret*,
died from a stroke, a tree felled by thunder,
buried in the American cemetery, Versailles.
If you go to see her, I think she will be gone,
battling banks over The Mount or taking a
leisurely stroll in the garden.

II.   EDNA

Edna St. Vincent Millay slipped the borders as she always did,
landing in Austerlitz, at Steepletop.
All her life she toppled barriers, busted through walls,
breaker of the rule and cracker of the safe.
She was middle-named after a hospital
and wanted to be called Vincent only.
Her principal countered by calling her only girls' names
beginning with "V" — Violet, Veronica, Victoria.
His authority held none for her.
Early on, she declared merry war on the world
and its contrivances.
She grew up a dirt poor-traveler
moving town to Northeast town with her mother and two sisters,
winning poetry awards from the age of 14.
She was freewheeling, wild, and outspoken,
living poor and jolly in the golden age
of glittering Greenwich Village.
She made a ferry crossing a fireworks celebration
and loved women at Vassar and beyond.
To burn her famous candle at both ends, she loved men, too.
Two men at a time, one possessing her above the waist
and one below, calling for some creativity or maybe none at all.
Her small, fluid body a ribbon unspooling,
her mouth an open valentine designed to kiss and rant.
Thomas Hardy said America had two attractions:
skyscrapers and Millay.
Her marriage of 26 years was open, her poet-lover

in the bedroom between hers and her husband's.
Weekends of wild parties at Steepletop
where once-innocent blueberries had grown.
Tennis courts with double entendres of "let" and "love."
But, quietly, a separate writing cabin
where her husband brought her meals.
He died, her only companion then alcohol.
The woman who had won the Pulitzer prize
for Poetry, the Frost Award,
who had been America's best-selling poet,
hid away with her booze and her books.
She drank life to the last shaky sip.
A trip on the first step started the free-fall down the stairway
where she lay for hours with a broken neck and heart.
Edna's sister came to Steepletop, stayed years, and moved nothing.
Her belongings in a shoebox, her dresses hung
on the bathtub's oval rod, holding the final curtain.
Mary Oliver lived there seven lucky years,
ordering Millay's papers, paving the way to her own Pulitzer.
You can take the Poet's Walk to Vincent's grave.
I think she will be gone, shimmering in a *boite*,
drinking in the Penthouse at Hardy's skyscraper,
waving down at us who barely light the match
much less burn the candle.

Whenever I See a Train, I Think of It Packed with Jews

Whenever I see a train,
I think of it packed with Jews.
Crying, starving, fighting,
pissing on the floor.
I know this is absurd.
The Orient Express does not stop at Dachau.
The train I see many times a day from my Pittsfield window
carries non-human freight.
But the mind is a murky and remembering thing.
And whenever I see a train,
I see Jews.

Baryshnikov

For the two hours
we watch Mark dance,
my eyes on the stage,
my eyes then on you
sitting in front of me,
head swiveling like a jumpy doll
on a dashboard.
Everything about you jets up:
spiky-blonde gelled hair
honed-arrow cheekbones
at-attention starched white collar
escaping a blue blazer.
You look loosely coiled to spring
poised to fly
ready to self-eject — RIGHT NOW! —
into the Boston night.

Eclipse Afternoon

The moon slides over the sun,
slivering it, playing a celestial joke,
creating a grey, sci-fi sky.
Approximately three — it seems to me —
three damn strange hours!
It feels like a '50s movie
and we're its street-bound stars.
The sky-bound stars emerge at noon.

Judy Jetson's salon empties into Massachusetts Avenue
like a washbasin from Noah's Ark.
Clients in all stages of disarrayed hair-care stare —
women in rollers like TV tubes, reeking of permanent solution;
men with half-haircuts tugging at their ears;
stylists swinging scissors.

We're all on the street like daylight drunks avoiding
the semi-shaded sun. (Newscasters tell you what to do if
your eye gets seared like a grilled grape.)
Students squint and turn, trying to solve the mystery.
A big black poodle careens by — loping, lost, berserk.
Leaves become cement crescents as strange treeshadows
are thrown onto the pavement, flung by a confused ball:
semi-sun, maybe moon, the heaven's plaything.

Boston Taxi Driver

With the hubbub of South Station,
packing in suitcases and settling into scratchy seats,
it takes me awhile to tune into the tone of your raised voice,
to wade through the thick words of angry Anglo-Arabic,
to get the gist, to understand you are angry with the deer
you hit on the highway last night,
a cool one in early Spring.

You offer to show me the fur-specked fender —
proof of the righteousness of your outrage —
when I only want to be your placid fare,
transported not into an argument but into Cambridge.
After ranting about the insurance company's disinterest,
you return to the wicked conniving deer,
whose small brain behind frightened brown eyes
plotted to plow into your instrument of income, knowing, no doubt,
you are an Arab to boot.
"It was sad for the deer, too, you know," I say, sure now
the meter will hit a jump bump or that stopping short,
he will hurl me into his uncaring block of a back.
"Yes," he says suddenly softening, his face caving in just a bit.
How good, healthy, and inevitable that we must part.

BOOKS BY DAN VALENTI

Baseball Comes Home: A History of the Baseball Hall
of Fame Game, 1940-2008 (2008)

Under a Grapefruit Sun: Red Sox Spring Training a Quarter Century Ago (2007)

Talking on Air: A Broadcaster's Life in Sports (with Ken Coleman, 2000)

Smoke in the Land of Orphans, a Novel (1994)

The Doctrine of Chance (1993)

Red Corvettes in Shadowland (1992)

A Man Like Him (1991)

TJ: My 26 Years in Baseball (with Tommy John, 1990)

Cactus League Roadtrip (1989)

Clout! The Top Home Runs in Baseball History (1989)

The Gunny (with R. Lee Ermey, 1989)

Grapefruit League Roadtrip (with Ken Coleman, 1988)

The Impossible Dream Remembered (with Ken Coleman, 1987)

Diary of a Sportscaster (with Ken Coleman, 1982)

From Florida to Fenway (1981)

Cities Journey (1981)

Red Sox: A Reckoning (1979)

EDITED BY DAN VALENTI

Vertically Coastal
by Jerri Chaplin (2011)

How Men See the World: Prize Winning Stories
by Paul Milenski (2011)

Triumph Over Cancer
by Ronald Sobecks, MD (2011)

Spring's Third Day
by Laura Gross (2010)

Divine Mercy: A Guide from Genesis to Benedict XVI
by Robert Stackpole (2009)

The Purest of All Lillies
by Donald Calloway (2008)

PLANET MEDIA BOOKS

ÉUROPOLIS

Planet Media Books, founded by Dan Valenti in 2010, publishes works from new and established authors in a wide range of topics including poetry, spirituality, art, philosophy, politics, economics, cooking, essays, nonfiction, and genre fiction. The press emphasizes creativity, fresh thought, quality writing, and ideas of important merit. Planet Media Books is an imprint of Planet Valenti (planetvalenti.com) in association with Európolis Management.

SPRING'S THIRD DAY
by Laura Gross

ISBN:

108 pages | $15.95

In Planet Media Books first title, poet Laura Gross delivers a collection of verse describing her metaphorical journey from the anger of deep winter to the hope of early spring. Gross' poems speak to those who have struggled against mighty odds to find peace of mind.

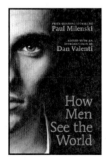

HOW MEN SEE THE WORLD
by Paul Milenski

ISBN:

200 pages | $19.95

Men see the world differently than women. Given this, what does it mean, anymore, to be a man ... or a boy? In this superb collection, award-winning writer Paul Milenski probes these questions with points and pincers, producing a message that is as relevant as now and as timeless as love.

Available at planetvalenti.com, danvalenti@verizon.net, tmbbooks.com, amazon.com, your local bookstore, and Planet Media Books, c/o Európolis Management
PO Box 1268, Stockbridge, MA 01262

ABOUT JERRI CHAPLIN

Jerri Chaplin is a certified poetry therapist and poet in Charleston, S.C. She divides her time between that city and Pittsfield, Mass. She served as the first poet-in-residence at the Gibbes Museum of Art in Charleston (1996). Her work has been widely published and anthologized, and her poems have won many awards, including from the Poetry Society of South Carolina. For two years, Chaplin served as vice president of the National Association for Poetry Therapy and received that organization's Outstanding Achievement Award (1999). She has given numerous readings from Pittsfield to Prague, including twice at Charleston's prestigious Piccolo Spoleto Festival. She is married to attorney/chef Peter Herman and has two sons, Geffen and Gabriel, and two grandsons, Fletcher and Forrest.